Kim and Cat

Written by Teresa Heapy

Illustrated by Morgan Huff

RISING ★ STARS

Tap!

Kim set up the paint pot.

Tip!

Kim set up the water pot.

Kim set up the glue pot.

Kim set up the glitter pot.

Kim and Cat tip and tap.

Talk about the story

Ask your child these questions:

1 What did Kim set up first?

2 What sound did the water pot make when it fell over?

3 Who knocked over the glitter pot?

4 Was Kim cross with Cat for joining in with her art activity?

5 Do you like using paint, glitter and glue to make pictures?

6 Which animal is your favourite to draw or paint?

Can your child retell the story in their own words?